GRAB & GRACE

OR

IT'S THE SECOND STEP

COMPANION AND SEQUEL TO
THE HOUSE BY THE STABLE

—

BY
CHARLES WILLIAMS

—

British Library Cataloguing-in-Publication Data
A catalogue record for this book is available from
the British Library

A HISTORY OF THE THEATRE

'The Theatre' is a collaborative form of fine art that uses live performers to present the experience of a real or imagined event. The performers may communicate this experience to the audience through combinations of gesture, speech, song, music, and dance, with elements of art, stagecraft and set design used to enhance the physicality, presence and immediacy of the experience. The specific place of the performance is also named by the word 'theatre' – derived from the Ancient Greek word *théatron*, meaning 'a place for viewing', itself from *theáomai*, meaning 'to see', 'watch' or 'observe'.

Modern Western theatre largely derives from ancient Greek drama, from which it borrows technical terminology, classification into genres, and many of its themes, stock characters, and plot elements. The city-state of Athens is where 'theatre' as we know it originated, as part of a broader culture of theatricality and performance in classical Greece that included festivals, religious rituals, politics, law, athletics, music, poetry, weddings, funerals, and symposia. Participation in the city-state's many festivals – and attendance at the City Dionysia as an audience member (or even as a participant in the theatrical productions) in particular, was an important part of citizenship.

The theatre of ancient Greece consisted of three types of drama: tragedy, comedy, and the satyr play (a form of tragicomedy, similar in spirit to the bawdy satire of burlesque). The origins of theatre in ancient Greece, according to Aristotle (384–322 BCE), the first theoretician of theatre, are to be found in the festivals that honoured Dionysus. These performances (the aforementioned City Dionysia) were held in semi-circular auditoria cut into hillsides, capable of seating 10,000–20,000 people. The stage consisted of a dancing floor (orchestra), dressing room and scene-building area (skene). Since the words were the most important part, good acoustics and clear delivery were paramount. The actors (always men) wore masks appropriate to the characters they represented, and each might play several parts.

Athenian tragedy (the oldest surviving form of tragedy) emerged sometime during the sixth century BCE, and flowered during the fifth century BCE – from the end of which it began to spread throughout the Greek world – and continued in popularity until the beginning of the Hellenistic period. Aeschylus, Sophocles, and Euripides were masters of the genre. The other side of the coin – Athenian comedy, is conventionally divided into three periods; 'Old Comedy', 'Middle Comedy', and 'New Comedy'. Old Comedy survives today largely in the form of the eleven surviving plays of Aristophanes, while Middle Comedy is largely lost (preserved only in a few relatively short fragments in authors such as Athenaeus of Naucratis). New Comedy is known primarily from the substantial papyrus fragments of Menander.

Western theatre developed and expanded considerably under the Romans. The theatre of ancient Rome was a thriving and diverse art form, ranging from festival performances of street theatre, nude dancing, and acrobatics, to the staging of Plautus's broadly appealing situation comedies, to the high-style, verbally elaborate tragedies of Seneca. Although Rome had a native tradition of performance, the Hellenization of Roman culture in the third century BCE had a profound and energizing effect on Roman theatre and encouraged the development of Latin literature of the highest quality for the stage. This tradition fed into the modern theatre we know today, and during the renaissance, theatre generally moved away from the poetic drama of the Greeks, and towards a more naturalistic prose style of dialogue. By the nineteenth century and the Industrial Revolution, this trend continued to progress.

In England, theatre was immensely popular, but took a big pause during 1642 and 1660 because of Cromwell's Interregnum. Prior to this, 'English renaissance theatre' was witnessed, with celebrated playwrights such as William Shakespeare, Christopher Marlowe and Ben Jonson. Under Queen Elizabeth, drama was a unified expression as far as social class was concerned, and the Court watched the same plays the commoners saw in the public playhouses. With the development of the private theatres, drama became more oriented towards the tastes and values of an upper-class audience however. By the later part of the reign of Charles I, few new plays were being written for the public theatres, which sustained themselves on the accumulated works of the previous decades. Theatre was now seen as something sinful and the Puritans tried very hard to drive it out of their society. Due to this stagnant period, once Charles II came back to the throne in 1660, theatre (among other arts) exploded with influences from France, and the wider continent.

The eighteenth century saw the widespread introduction of women to the stage – a development previously unthinkable. These women were looked at as celebrities (also a newer concept, thanks to ideas on individualism that were beginning to be born in Renaissance Humanism) but on the other hand, it was still very new and revolutionary. Comedies were full of the young and very much in vogue, with the storyline following their love lives: commonly a young roguish hero professing his love to the chaste and free minded heroine near the end of the play, much like Sheridan's *The School for Scandal*. Many of the comedies were fashioned after the French tradition, mainly Molière (the great comedic playwright), again harking back to the French influence of the King and his court after their exile.

After this point, there was an explosion of theatrical styles. Throughout the nineteenth century, the popular theatrical forms of Romanticism, melodrama, Victorian burlesque and the well-made plays of Scribe and Sardou gave way to the problem plays of Naturalism and Realism; the farces of Feydeau; Wagner's operatic *Gesamtkunstwerk*; musical theatre (including Gilbert and Sullivan's operas); F. C. Burnand's, W. S. Gilbert's and Wilde's drawing-room comedies; Symbolism; proto-Expressionism in the late works of August Strindberg and Henrik Ibsen; and Edwardian musical comedy. The list continues! These trends continued through the twentieth century in the realism of Stanislavski and Lee Strasberg, the political theatre of Erwin Piscator and Bertolt Brecht, the so-called Theatre of the Absurd of Samuel Beckett and Eugène Ionesco, and the rise of American and British musicals.

Theatre itself has an incredibly long history, and despite the massive proliferation of theatrical styles and mediums – it essentially owes its existence to the ancient Greeks and the Romans. The three main genres; tragedy, comedy and satyre, continue to influence plot themes, directing, writing and acting, with frequent and fascinating interrelations and overlaps. As a genre, it remains as popular today as it has ever been, and continues as a massive influence on popular culture more broadly. It is hoped that the current reader enjoys this book on the subject.

CHARLES WILLIAMS

Charles Walter Stansby Williams was born in London in 1886. He dropped out of University College London in 1904, and was hired by Oxford University Press as a proof-reader, quickly rising to the position of editor. While there, arguably his greatest editorial achievement was the publication of the first major English-language edition of the works of the Danish philosopher Søren Kierkegaard.

Williams began writing in the twenties and went on to publish seven novels. Of these, the best-known are probably *War in Heaven* (1930), *Descent into Hell* (1937), and *All Hallows' Eve* (1945) – all fantasies set in the contemporary world. He also published a vast body of well-received scholarship, including a study of Dante entitled *The Figure of Beatrice* (1944) which remains a standard reference text for academics today, and a highly unconventional history of the church, *Descent of the Dove* (1939). Williams garnered a number of well-known admirers, including T. S. Eliot, W. H. Auden and C. S. Lewis. Towards the end of his life, he gave lectures at Oxford University on John Milton, and received an honorary MA degree. Williams died almost exactly at the close of World War II, aged 58.

GRAB AND GRACE
OR
IT'S THE SECOND STEP

(Companion and sequel to
THE HOUSE BY THE STABLE)

CHARACTERS

PRIDE

HELL

GABRIEL

FAITH

MAN

GRACE

GRAB AND GRACE

The scene as before. Enter HELL *and* PRIDE, *bedraggled and tired;*
HELL carrying a large bundle

PRIDE. No rest? no comfortable house?
    These lands are as empty of homes as our bag of food—
    yet I should know this place!
HELL.   Why surely this—
    yes, look, in this crook of the hills,
    look, here is Man's house once more!
    After this hundred years we have been wandering
    through the malignant lands, to think we have come
    again to your old home. What think you, Pride?
    Might it not be possible to find a rest here?
PRIDE. Why, it would be worth while to try; I
    and you too were so beshouted and bevenomed
    by that slug-slimy Gabriel that we lost our heads
    and ran too soon. Man cannot have forgotten;
    few do; their faithfulness to me is astonishing.
    Shall we knock, do you think?
HELL.   Prink yourself first.
PRIDE. This accurst mud!
HELL.   That dress will not provoke him
    under your yoke again.
PRIDE.   Look and see
    if we have anything better in our odds and ends.
        [HELL *opens the bundle, and they poke about: fragments*
        fall out]
PRIDE. I cannot think why we carry all this.
    What is this red stuff?
HELL.   A little of Abel's blood.
    A drop of that in a drink gives a man heartburn.

PRIDE.   And this?

HELL.   Take care; a bit of Adam's tooth
    that he broke on the first fruit out of Paradise.
    He has had neuralgia in his jaws ever since.

PRIDE.   And this—thistledown?

HELL.   The kiss of Judas.

PRIDE.   Judas?

HELL.   You were sick of malignant plague when it happened—
    but the child whom Man sheltered when we had gone
    grew, and grew spoiled, and Judas, one of his friends,
    encouraged Man to kill him in a sudden brawl.
    There is no time now to tell you all.

PRIDE.   All
    meaning that when Man had got rid of me
    things did not go so well as Gabriel thought?
    You fool, Hell, why did you not tell me
    all this sooner?

HELL.   I had forgotten; my fits
    make me dull. We are not what we were;
    neither you nor I have ever been the same
    since the great earthquake and the talking flame.

PRIDE.   Hell,
    did we not hear that Man had a changed heart?
    I am sure that some antipodean rumour
    reached us of his altered humour; that he likes now
    prayer and servile monochromatic designs.
    Draggled decency might better suit us?

HELL.   I will say, looking at our bag, it would be easier.
    May not you be converted as well as he?
    Try that style: [*He grabbles about*] look, what of this?
                 [*He holds up a dirty rough clo*
    How of this for a man's earthenware embrace
    and a chaste kiss? [*She puts it on*] Your very face looks holy.

PRIDE.   What is it?

HELL.   Devil knows; the original figleaves, I should think.
You will need a belt. [*He holds one up*] Jezebel's?

PRIDE.   My dear, too bright.
What's that?

HELL.   The cord with which Judas hanged himself,
afterwards used to tie Peter to his cross.

PRIDE. That is the very thing; give it here.

[*She looks at herself*
I don't know who Peter was, but if
he was crucified, it is something anyone might be proud of.
Pride in a nutshell! [*She wriggles*] with the shell of the nut inside.
Hist, someone is coming!

HELL [*throwing the things in the bag*]. Is it Man?

PRIDE. No; it's a woman; what the devil—

HELL.   Chut!
There's Gabriel! Out of sight till we find out more!

[*They hide. Enter* FAITH, *meeting* GABRIEL. *She is dressed
as brightly and sophisticatedly as is possible*]

FAITH. Good-morning, Gabriel: where is my lord?

GABRIEL.   Madam,
he was in the stables just now, but I think he has gone
back with Grace to the house.

FAITH.   The stables?

GABRIEL.   Yes.
He has not been there much since the Holy One died,
but this morning something stirred.

FAITH.   A word in a song!
O to-day is such a morning as I love,
cloudy and cool; one feels rather than sees
the sun heavenly: he is distilled in the air,
and my heart filled with his future; in the dawn
I made a new song, and would fain sing it,
if Man my lord were free to hear.

3

GABRIEL.   Madam,
  could he do better than listen to Faith's songs?
FAITH. Well, to be frank, that depends; but thank you
  for the kind thought. I will go and find him out.
  O loveliness, to feel day in the dawn!

                                                              [*Ex*

PRIDE [*aside to* HELL]. And will you tell me who Faith is, an
  what
  Faith, in that dress, is doing in Man's house,
  and I in this—shroud?
HELL [*aside*].   Not so loud; hush!
GABRIEL [*looking round*]. You need not trouble yourselves to hus
      your smell
  would give you away; surely it is Hell and Pride?
  The old obscene graveyard stink; I think
  honest anger and brutal lust smell pure
  beside you.
PRIDE.   Stew-faced bully!
HELL.   Sister, be at ease.
  Once he had power even over us for an hour,
  but not twice thus, not twice.
  Abuse you he may; he cannot turn you away.
  He must let Man choose now for himself.
PRIDE. Are you sure you are right?
HELL.   Of course——
GABRIEL.   Of course he is right.
  I could be, were angels ever other than glad,
  a little sad to see you with more tricks.
  But now Man has friends if he will,
  and if you can cheat him, why, you must.
  I can do no more than tell him who you are.
PRIDE. I will tell him that myself.
GABRIEL.   So do.
  You seem perhaps more true than most

4

sins to their nature—and so catch more.

Double temptation when a sin pretends to be truthful.

HELL. No, sir. We need not trouble you to announce us.

GABRIEL. No need; here is Man.

[MAN *enters with* GRACE

HELL.   Now!

PRIDE.   Get away!

Much better for me to be alone. Man!

MAN [*to* GRACE]. We will build then; I have decided that.

The cottages are clammy; we need several more

and more to the mind of those likely to live there.

First, we must find an architect.

GRACE.   O sir,

I know a fine one, in design and execution

better than any; all the worlds praise

his work these many days.

MAN.   Who then is he?

GRACE. He is called the Spirit; those who know his degree

add a worshipful title and say the Holy Spirit:

that as you choose.

MAN.   The Holy Spirit? good.

We will ask him to come while I am in the mood,

which passes so quickly and then all is so dull. ·

GRACE. Sir, purposes last.

MAN.   Yes, but heavily.

Madam?

PRIDE.'   Man!

MAN. Do I—ought I—to know. . . ? I have met few

of your veiled kind; yet——

PRIDE.   Man!

MAN. By my soul, it is Pride.

PRIDE.   Yes. [*A pause*] Do you grieve?

Would you have me leave, without a word changed?

I will, if you say go.

MAN.   No; stay.
   Where have you been? I have not seen you since——
PRIDE. Since your servant told—yes; they *were* lies.
   Though indeed I was foolish then, now more wise.
   But to mistake folly for foul thought,
   to drive me out while you slept! Have you sometimes kept
   a thought of me?—no; that is folly again.
   I am professed now to other vows,
   as my dress shows. I have even changed my name
   and am called Self-Respect.
MAN.   What, you are one
   of Immanuel's people?
PRIDE [*drooping*].   He has a use for all.
        [*She turns aside and gets near to* HELL; *then aside*
   What was her name? quick, the great sinner,
   the woman.
HELL.   Mary Magdalene.
PRIDE [*returning*].   Even Mary Magdalene—
   and so for me, who did not (I may well say)
   sin as much as she—and was she more beautiful?
   Once, dear Man, you thought me well enough.
MAN. It is astonishing to see you; you have not changed.
   The same lovely eyes under that hood.
   It is good to see you once more, my own Pride;
   no, I must call you my own Self-Respect.
   It is what I will try to remember.
      [GRACE *whistles.* PRIDE *and* MAN *turn away.* GRACE *and*
      GABRIEL *speak to* HELL]
GRACE. And here is poor old Hell!
HELL.   Little tin trumpet,
   how do you know me?
GABRIEL.   O we of heaven
   know you all. This boy, whom we call Grace—
   he is part of Faith's household, and she of Man's—

6

is older than you. Indeed, he does not look it,
but your travels in the malignant lands have aged you
more than our millenia.

GRACE. A thousand years
being as a day. Poor Hell, time to you
is a sorry plod-plod; even Man knows better,
but Hell of all pedestrians is the most tired.
And why are you here, little brother?

HELL. What is that to you?
May we not talk to Man without your leave?

GABRIEL. Unfortunately, yes.

GRACE. And is she doing it now!

PRIDE. And tell me, dear Man, how you are faring in Religion.

MAN. Well, I am trying to lead the Christian life.
It is not easy, is it, Gabriel?

GABRIEL. Sir,
I do not think you have found it too difficult.

PRIDE. To lead the Christian life is always difficult.
How we have to work! digging, building,
giving alms, prayer. Do you pray much?

MAN. A good deal. Gabriel, what do you mean?

GABRIEL. Sir, only that you have been constantly helped.
This boy Grace does most of the work.

MAN. I know Grace has been useful, but to say
he does most—I was up as early as he
and as bustling round my property.

PRIDE. That I am sure.
I know how dextrous and diligent you always are.

MAN. I will give praise where praise is due, but something
is due to me.

PRIDE. Much, indeed.

GABRIEL. Sir——

GRACE. Chut, Gabriel; you will never defeat her so.
Do not argue; make her come out with herself

quickly; believe me, it is your only way.
Call Faith; she is better than you at the game,
and can frame a neater trap, woman to woman.

[GABRIEL *goes out*

PRIDE. It is no credit to any cause not to know
if one has kept its laws well. Flaws
will come, but when one has minded laws—why,
then a certain proper pride may grow.
I have taken Self-Respect for my new name
to adjust properly praise and blame, to keep
myself in mind as a true centre for myself.

MAN.   True.
One has more belief, so, in what one can do.

PRIDE. That is it: no weakness, no false meekness.
This humility is too much praised.
One may look at oneself, I hope, without sin.
You, my Man, can keep your thought so poised
that any noised silliness does not hurt.
You are pious—good! but it is *you* who are pious.

MAN. I had not thought of that. Faith sings
only about Immanuel and what he does.
That brings a sense of vacancy sometimes.

PRIDE. Yes: one needs at first a kind of defence
against even heaven. Perfection comes slowly;
and we must not be too holy all at once.

[*Enter* FAITH *and* GABRIEL

FAITH. Good-morning, my lord.

MAN.   Good-morning, Faith.

PRIDE [*to* MAN].   This
is another friend of yours?

MAN.   Her name is Faith.
She was a friend of Immanuel, the child born
the night you went. . . . O well, Pride—
I beg your pardon; it is old habit in me—

8

we need not go into all that now.
There was a misunderstanding of what he meant
and a tussle—you, my dear, will understand
there was something to be said on my side;
but anyhow—it was all rather unfortunate—he died.
But he left with me these two friends,
she and the boy Grace. Let me introduce——

PRIDE. She will despise me, Man. I am poor
and of no account, but I have enough respect
for myself not to push in among the elect,
among—look at her clothes!—my ostensible betters.

MAN. Clothes—nonsense. You look very nice—
quiet and . . . becoming.

PRIDE.   Man!

MAN.   Well, I
have you in my mind as you were when . . . but come;
it suits you. You are my own Self-Respect,
and this is my own Faith; you must know each other.

                           [GRACE *whistles*

Faith, this is an old friend of mine,
called—do I say Sister?

PRIDE.   Yes—I suppose,
Sister.

        [*She clings to his hand and looks deep into his eyes*

MAN. . . . called . . . Sister Self-Respect.
And this, dear friend, is Faith.

PRIDE.   Pleased to meet you.

FAITH [*coldly*]. Good-morning.

PRIDE.   Is it not a good morning?
[*To* MAN] This house was always good in the spring days.

FAITH. You have known Man a long while?

PRIDE.   Very long.
[*To* MAN] Of course, times change; I know now
you have other friends.

FAITH.   Yes.

MAN.   No.

You must not say so; at least, if I have,
I do not forget my old.

FAITH.   It seems not;
especially when they return in a neat religious
habit, and are prettily disposed to public prayer.

PRIDE. What do you mean—public?

FAITH.   I do not mean
praying with others present, but rather that sedate
praying to oneself, with oneself too as listener;
a ubiquitous trinity of devotion the temple-Pharisee
practised long and successfully.

PRIDE.   At least I
earned my lodging here by a decent return—
by something other than songs; night was my time.

FAITH. Yes; *my* joys encourage sight,
accuracy, and reason.

PRIDE.   My kisses were accurate:
Man enjoyed them and himself and me.
I did not confine myself to singing him songs.

MAN. O now, Self-Respect, they are beautiful songs.
Everyone to his own gift . . . indeed,
you always had beautiful shoulders.

PRIDE.   Have I not?
as beautiful bare as hers bundled on Sundays?

                [GRACE *whistles.* HELL *creeps towards hi*

I am sorry, Man. I did not mean to snap.
I had better go.

MAN.   O no, you must not go.
We shall all be great friends—I, Man,
and his Self-Respect and his Faith: why not?

FAITH. His Self-Respect and his Faith! No. Man,
you must make up your mind. There is a strong feud

renewed for centuries, from our very making, between
this lady and myself.
PRIDE.   There is indeed—
between my pleasure and your procrastination,
you promising what you do not pay,
and I paying what I need not bother to promise.
                              [GRACE *whistles*
HELL [*to* GRACE]. Stop that noise!
GRACE.   Noise yourself;
Adam called the birds on that note
while you were squeaking and squealing among the crocodiles.
O crocodiles' guiles and smiles and wiles,
when Hell styles himself a judge of music.
                   [HELL *threatens him.* GRACE *trips him.*
Heels up, gossamer!
MAN.   Less noise over there!
Grace, keep yourself quiet in your own place.
Now, let us agree here to be friends.
Love puts all ends at one, and spends
much to do it: come, wine for a pledge.
Gabriel!
GABRIEL.   Sir, the ladies will never agree.
If you wish to turn Faith out of doors . . .
MAN. What! my friend's friend! Immanuel's friend . . .
why do you remind me? No; I promised; I am firm.
GABRIEL. Then send Pride away.
MAN.   O now, Gabriel,
I owe her, after all, a great deal,
and she understands me, she soothes me.
PRIDE.   I am not Pride.
Indeed, Gabriel, I have forgotten all that.
I am the old woman on the new way:
look at me, a demure modest Self-Respect;
nothing spectacular or dishonourable about *me*.

Of course, I am not *blind*; I cannot help
noticing where sinners thrive, or where they sin,
or how parasites and amateur prostitutes are dressed.
FAITH. The professional always hates being outclassed—
I agree there: for the word—let it stand.
Our feud, on my side, is too deep
to use abuse. I say I will not sit down
nor eat nor drink nor sleep in the same house
with—Self-Respect. I do not and will not know her.
PRIDE. And I—*I!*—used to be called Pride!
Is this your charity, you over-painted, over-powdered,
verminous haunch of a hag-bone! you snorting porcupine,
pet of a fellow whose hands never kept his head!
Why, you dilly-down doveling, you mincing mosquito——
    [GRACE *whistles.* HELL *runs at him; they dodge out, shouting*
      while PRIDE *is screaming and* FAITH *speaking*]
FAITH. I will not abuse you. I simply will not know you.
MAN [*shouting*]. Silence! Gabriel, keep the house quiet!
See what Grace is doing and tell him not to.
And now, you two, am I to say nothing?
Am I not to have my own way?
You shall behave in this house, both of you,
as if I were someone.
PRIDE.   O Man,
that is right! keep us in order; send us to prayer.
Rebuke us! Have I hurt you? O beat me
if I disturb you! I am only yours—
and of course God's; but I *am* wholly yours
in a new love, if you choose!
MAN.   This fiddle-faddle!
Argument in, argument out. Man
will have his way sometimes; if I choose
you shall both stop with me, stop you shall.
I will tie you up, Pride!

PRIDE. Anything, anything!

[GABRIEL *has been looking out*

GABRIEL. Sir, look!

MAN. What is the matter now?
What are they doing there? who is the fellow?
Why, it is Hell! Was he here too?

GABRIEL. He is throttling Grace!

MAN. He is throwing him into the lake—
he will drown; it has no bottom. Hi!
Hell there, Hell, leave him alone!
Grace, we are coming!

[*He runs out*

GABRIEL. Sir, Grace can swim;
indeed, there is very little Grace cannot do—
for example—get out of a bottomless pit.
Well, it is proper that Man should run fast
when heaven seems in danger; heaven has done
as much for him.

[*He goes leisurely out*

FAITH. O sister, sister, now we may talk sense.
You must find it exhausting always to be
on guard, watching every word. Myself,
help though I have and celestial succour,
I am glad sometimes when my sister Hope
takes my place for a night; and I can speak
right and direct; the muscles in my face
are controlled naturally and not by sheer work
to please Man's variable moods. Poor Man,
he is a sweet darling, but O I wish
he had an adult intelligence.

PRIDE. You can drop this feud
when Man is not here!

FAITH. He is a born mimic,
and therefore I must refuse to have you here,

or you would catch him with one or the other ruse.
Alone, we may leave it to God.

PRIDE.   Why are you so bent
 to have him? he will never do *you* good.

FAITH. To obey Immanuel is in my blood; and he
 chooses so. But how will Man serve *you*?

PRIDE. O yes; when we have him—as we shall;
 you will call one day to an empty house;
 anything else is not possible; well, then,
 while your songs echo and re-echo, none
 to mark them, except perhaps the sun in heaven,
 think that Man is another vagrant I
 and Hell shall sometimes meet where the sky
 has no sun, in the clammy malignant lands
 that Hell once made.

FAITH.   And now finds
 everywhere terribly following him; even here.
 O I know well wherever you go,
 he and you, you sooner or later feel
 the air of the cold iceberg or hot oasis
 breaking into the same clamminess, the same
 disgusting invisible froth against the skin—
 ugh! every wind, every rain-drop,
 every grateful beam crawling and sticky.

       [HELL *creeps in behind her, making signs to* PRIDE

PRIDE [*getting nearer*]. Yes; we shall have a companion then, to bear
 the bag over there of the odds and ends
 we stole out of his house; in a dim mist
 he shall stumble after us, afraid to lose even us,
 or sometimes be pricked by me or kicked by Hell
 forward before us, among the shallow pools
 or the miry grass under the malignant trees
 where the baboons sit and scratch and yowl.
 There with us tramping and trapesing for ever.

FAITH. Poor wretch! but you haven't . . .

> [HELL *seizes her*. PRIDE *covers her mouth*

HELL. I have thrown Grace into the lake; quick.
  Shove this cloth in her mouth; tie it.
  If we can hide her we may lure Man
  out of his house into the malignant lands.
  Keep him till the sun sets and leave me alone
  to draw him down among the pits and pools.

PRIDE. Twist her arms behind her: use your fist.

> [HELL *strikes at* FAITH; *she dodges*; *he hits* PRIDE

  Damn! O anyhow: be quick.

HELL. Give me that cord; they will be a few minutes.
  Hang on to her wrists while I tie her legs.

PRIDE [*panting*]. She is so supple.

HELL.   All right. Now—
  in front then—pull! there. Where shall we put her?
  behind that tree?

PRIDE.   No; Hell, the bag!
  the bag! throw our things behind the tree,
  anyhow, in a heap, and then have her in.

HELL. Excellent! empty it. Now—over her head!

> [FAITH *digs him in the stomach*

  Ouch! Her hands are about as delicate as iron.
  There . . . steady . . . *there*. That settles Faith.

PRIDE. She can have her feud all to herself there,
  and fill her belly with her own gaudiness.

HELL.   Here—
  help tie it under her feet; so.
  I hear them; quick; carry it over here.

> [*They carry the bag to the back*. MAN, GABRIEL, *and* GRACE
> *come in*]

MAN. Hell, this is outrageous. He might have been drowned.
  O yes, I know he is a tiresome boy.

I am sure he provoked me often, his jokes
and his insolence, but to treat him so—

HELL. I would have seen to it he came to no hurt,
had you not been by: since you were—
But I was rash. I agree I did wrong.
I apologize—gentleman to gentleman. As for him—
here, lad, and another time watch your tongue.
Catch!

[*He throws him something*

GABRIEL.   One of the thirty pieces, was it?
Grace will win them all back, one day,
and not by playing dice.

MAN.   Well, now . . .
where is Faith?

PRIDE.   Gone into the house.
She would not even take the air with me;
she preferred her own room to my company.
[*aside to* HELL] For the devil's sake give me a better belt;
I can't keep my things together.

HELL [*aside*].   Jezebel's?
It is all we have.

PRIDE [*aside*].   Any damn thing.
Your friends, dearest Man, are a little difficult.
Faith is rude to me and Grace to my brother—
not that I mind—and I (poor soul!) thought
just for once I would replace the cord
of my habit with a little brightness, my old lightness
of heart took me so to be with you.

[*She puts on the bel*

Does it look silly?

MAN.   No, but more like you.

PRIDE. Of course, I do forgive your friend. You know
that is where Religion helps. One can forgive.
Is it not pleasant, dearest, to forgive others?

It is far sweeter than anger, more satisfying.
Lying in bed at night, I love to think
how many sinners poor little Self-Respect
has forgiven—even in a week or so. To be oneself
is always to find how much better than others
one surprisingly is. I take no credit,
of course, for that, though indeed, Man,
you loved me: did I seem—never mind.
You loved me.

MAN.   Yes.

PRIDE.   It was something of a joy.
Did you not feel yourself to be noble then?

MAN. Yes.

PRIDE.   O come for a little; come!
No, not in the house—out here,
away from all your people. Yes indeed,
I know we now are otherwise turned
and so will be; but an hour—come!
You shall be true to Faith and I to my vows;
only a little walk, a little murmur,
a reverie, a day-dream, a distant noon-glimpse
of our past joy, a thing forgotten but
for just this one companioned glance,
this twy-memoried gleam far below.
Come.

MAN.   I have never been able to forget you.

PRIDE.   Come.

MAN. O how the blood runs quicker! O—
Pride, Faith's songs are very sweet
but strange, alien with that accent, sweet
terribly, but to be with you is to lose terror,
to lose the beauty that strips me of comfort. Pride,
that is a dull dark dress you are wearing;
your belt shows it up; it is not like you.

PRIDE. We will see if we can find something brighter,
    more to my lord's liking; we might. Come.

> [GRACE *has been poking up among* HELL's *properties. He plays a tune*]

    Would you not like to see me? no, say,
    there is no dress for Pride as beautiful as she,
    as you used to. Only for a moment; only for joy
    of the memory; then back to Immanuel and Faith.
    Kiss me and say so. Kiss me.

MAN. Hark a minute. Who is that playing?
    It is that strange distant song
    which pricks a point of fire in each joint.
    Grace, what have you there?

GRACE.   This, my lord?
    I found it hidden in a heap behind a tree.
    It is one of the dulcimers Nebuchadnezzar's orchestra
    played at the grand show of the Three-in-the-Fire,
    who became, unexpectedly, Four.

MAN.   How Four?
    Is that the song's name?

GRACE.   O my lord,
    the tale is old: it was one of Immanuel's doings.
    Faith afterwards made a good song
    on the dance of the Four-in-the-Fire. Hear me play,
    and see if your heart does not move to the steps of the Fourth.
    Sit, my lord; here is something to sit on.

> [*He begins to roll the bag out*

PRIDE *and* HELL. Leave that alone!

PRIDE. Man, make your servants leave untouched
    Our few poor belongings. It is my bag
    and my brother's dulcimer.

GRACE.   Nebuchadnezzar's dulcimer;
    stolen like Abel's blood and Adam's tooth

and all the rest, from this very house.
I only recover it.
GABRIEL.   Indeed, sir, you have
   a right to your own antiques—to give to Hell
   if you wish, but even Hell must not steal.
   Your museum was unique, but that bag holds much.
   Roll it nearer, Grace.
HELL.   Leave it alone.
   That dulcimer never came from the bag.
PRIDE. Yes; it is mine.
HELL.   Yes; but not from the bag.
   That is full.
GABRIEL.   Ah but what fills it?
   Tell me that, Hell. And look at it!
   It is moving.
GRACE [*striking an attitude and sepulchrally*]. And where is Faith?
HELL.   How do I know?
PRIDE. Back in the house.
MAN.   Something is inside the bag.
PRIDE. Dear Man, only my own pet scorpions.
   I cannot bear to leave them behind; one day
   I will show them to you, but not just now.
MAN. Scorpions! no scorpion ever moved like that.
   What have you got there?
GRACE.   Aha!
HELL.   Man,
   We did not come here to be insulted.
                              [GRACE *whistles*
GABRIEL. The bag, sir, is trying to attract your attention.
   I submit that the whole affair is so suspicious
   you have a right to open it.
HELL.   No!
PRIDE.   No!
                    [*The blade of a knife appears*

GRACE. Ladies and gentlemen, observe the scorpion's sting.
Little sister, your scorpions may stab you yet.
MAN. It is opening all of itself. Nothing like this
has ever happened in my house before.
GRACE.   My lord,
nothing like my lady Faith and I
ever happened in anyone's house before.
Adored be the Omnipotence for ever and ever!
> [FAITH'S *head appears through the cut*. GABRIEL *and* GRACE
> *run to help her out*]
GRACE. Faith in a bag is Faith at her best!
GABRIEL.   No;
even Faith must flag when she is stifled,
and Faith with vision is wiser than Faith without.
FAITH. Faith—and Faith may say so—is pretty well smothered.
O this old smell of Man's horrors
clings to the cloth, the beastly evidence
of things unhoped and undesired,
the present substance of things past and unseen.
Pah!   [*She stands up*
MAN. Faith, who has done this? I vow
I will now do justice. I keep promise—
I? no; I do not see my way
or what to say, but I swear the promise shall be kept
that I made Immanuel when he leapt into heaven—
mocking (O I know it! I know it!) my serious sin.
Tell me, who has done this?
PRIDE.   One
who will finish her work!
> [*She snatches a dagger from* HELL's *belt and leaps at* FAITH
HELL.   Fool, leave it alone!
She is immortal like us! O imbecile!
> [FAITH *catches* PRIDE *and bends her back, twisting the hand
> holding the knife*]

20

MAN. Drop that!

[*He makes a movement forward*

FAITH.   Stop there, Man.
She has challenged me alone and I alone
will take the challenge. Since you will not choose
by honour or love, will you take the mere fact?
Will you believe in the power?

[HELL *moves;* MAN *seizes him*

MAN.   A little else!
There shall be none beside to interfere;
that at least I can do!

FAITH.   Blessed Man,
I will swear at the Judgement that you helped me here.
So, Pride, so.

[MAN *wrestles with* HELL

PRIDE.   Ah, beast!
Help me, Hell!

HELL.   Pride, help me!

GABRIEL.   Grace,
would not your quick touch finish the trick?

GRACE. I have brought them to a clear field! now yield
the weaker! well I know who that will be.
O Man, well thrown! poor Hell!

[MAN *throws* HELL *and puts his foot on him*

MAN. Well sung, Grace! had you not found
and struck the dulcimer, I should have fallen to folly
deeper and darker, and my Faith died.
O the sight of the knife cured all.
Does she need help?

GABRIEL.   Probably not. I have known
Faith live and thrive in odd places
by her own mere valour. Look now.

[*In the fina stress* PRIDE *breaks down; the dagger is twisted
from her, and she falls*]

21

GRACE. Well done, Faith! well done, Man! So.

[*He picks up the dagge.*

I thought so; Cain's old obsidian knife!
What will you do with them now, my lord?

MAN.   I?

What have I to do with giving sentence?

[*He moves away.* HELL *rises*

It seems to me that when I say *I*
or when I think myself someone I am always wrong.

GABRIEL. Sir, you have known that all the time
if you let yourself think.

GRACE.   O chut, chut!

Gabriel, you archangels are so stern—
let our sweet lord make his own discoveries:
do not be so severe on his human reason
you with your communicated heavenly intuitions!

GABRIEL. I too have—never mind. You are right, Grace.
This is not the place or the time for rebuke.
Sir, it is true that for ever in this house
you hold the high, the low, and the middle justice
over all things; yet, as Hell said,
they are immortals; they cannot be put to death.
I do not advise perpetual prison here,
not trusting Pride—nor, sir, to be frank,
thinking you would have much chance against her.
We have seen——

GRACE.   Gabriel! Come off your grand angelic
passion for instruction. This is Man's affair;
I would swear (if I could) he would do himself right,
and us.

GABRIEL.   Very well. Sir, what will you do?

MAN. Do? it is they have done their last and worst.

[GRACE *whistles.* MAN *looks at him*

GRACE [*hastily*]. My lord, I am sorry; that was old habit.

When I am sceptical I always whistle,
and as for doing their *last*—forgive me; speak.

MAN. Let them go then to their own place.
Up and out!

> [PRIDE *rises; she and* HELL *look at each other; she screams*

PRIDE.   O no, no!
Man, I will repent, I will do better,
I will be good one day—no, to-day.
Do not send me out to the malignant lands;
do not send me out with Hell! Save me!

GABRIEL. Sister, it was your choice.

PRIDE.   No, never;
not with him. O Man, Man——

GABRIEL. Man is not to be asked now; he judged.
The execution is remitted to us. We
are his household; we wear his livery; we do his will.
The Mercy of God takes Man at his word
and enforces it, by us who obey him on earth. Go.

PRIDE. Man, I loved you——

GABRIEL.   Loved! O little sister,
if anything was wanting, that has finished all.
Call Love in and Pride is lost.

HELL. Come, sister; the journey begins again.

PRIDE. No, no! [*She rushes from one to the other;* MAN *hides his
face*] Save me! You have not gone,
you have not walked with him among the pools,
beyond the baboons and the crocodiles, beyond all
but the quicksands that never quite swallow us, under a moon
that never quite lights us, in the death that never quite dies,
and *he*——

GABRIEL.   Is this Pride?

PRIDE.   No, no.
No Pride! O if you had carried that bag—

the things we stole from you are beautiful beside
the things he can fill it with.
FAITH.   But what does he *do*?
PRIDE. Denatures.
GABRIEL.   Denatures!
FAITH.   O horrible! O
    God, pitiful God, have mercy on all!

[*There is a pause*

PRIDE. Yes. Hell. I am coming to you, Hell.

[*She stumbles towards him*

HELL [*softly*]. The bag, Pride; do not forget the bag.
    It will be filled soon down there,
    and now it is your turn to carry it—harlot!
PRIDE. Yes, Hell. [*She fetches it*] Here it is, Hell.
HELL. Come then. [*To the others*] We will be back presently.

[*They go out*

GABRIEL. So. That is done. Now——
FAITH and GRACE. Sh-h!
GRACE. Gabriel, there must be many things in the house
    waiting for you. The silver needs polishing
    perhaps; or the accounts—think of the accounts!
GABRIEL. Grace, if you were not a Divine gift——
GRACE. Yes, but I am——
GABRIEL.   You are. If you were not——
GRACE. I know; I know; you said so. The silver, Gabriel,
    the accounts! the dinner! We must dine, Gabriel!
    While Man is on earth, he must dine;
    and I do better myself on a certain nourishment.
    Remember Cana of Galilee!
GABRIEL.   Cana of Galilee!
    Really . . .

[*He goes out*

FAITH.   It is the second step that counts.
    My lord, I can say nothing now to cheer

24

a broken heart; only that mine too
broke; we are not adult till then—O
we are not even young; the second step,
the perseverance into the province of death,
is a hard thing; then there is no return.
Most dear lord, if I could do you good,
I would; as it is——

MAN.   O Faith, Faith, I loved her.

FAITH. Yes.

MAN.   I loved her; God knows how I loved her.

FAITH. Therefore God shall make all things well—
    O agony! O bounteous and fell judgement!— . . .
    When you want me, if you want me, I will come
    quicker than you can think. The Peace be with you,
    and Love which is all substance in all things made.

                                    [*She goes out*

MAN. A second step . . . a second step in love . . .
    What, O almighty Christ, what of the third?

www.ingramcontent.com/pod-product-compliance
Lightning Source LLC
Chambersburg PA
CBHW031221090426
42740CB00009B/1259